Looking Back

The University of Manchester

THE UNIVERSITY
of MANCHESTER

First published in Great Britain in 1996 by
The University of Manchester,
Oxford Road, Manchester M13 9PL

Copyright©1996 The University of Manchester

ISBN 0 906107 69 5

*Front cover photograph: The Whitworth Hall and its
neighbours dominate a cobbled and traffic-free
Oxford Road, 1908.*

*Back cover photograph: An unidentified Magritte-like figure
leaves the soot-blackened John Owens Building behind him.
ca.1960*

Printed in Great Britain by Shanley's Colour Printers Ltd.

Foreword

As you would expect of an institution which is almost 150 years old, there is a mass of artefacts hidden away at The University of Manchester, which record both its development and the famous events which have occurred there, since 1851.

It became apparent at a very early stage in the research for this book, that the University has a highly-distinguished history that is virtually unknown to the majority of its staff, students, graduates and friends. To discover the famous names that have been associated with the place, and to learn the background to its evolution, has been a fascinating experience. The difficult task of accurately recording the full history of the University has been undertaken at the 50th and 100th anniversaries of foundation, and will be repeated in 2001. In this short photographic record, we give a selective and condensed version of that story.

Limitations in the materials available, and the difficulty in tying names and events to an image, have restricted the areas covered in this book. Similarly, many of the photographs included here were sourced from the estates archive of the University, and therefore concentrate on buildings, rather than people. However, the changes brought about by the expansion of the campus to its present size are extraordinary, and will interest anybody who has ever been connected with the University.

Compiled by:

Matthew Wainwright, Registrar & Secretary's Department

The University of Manchester

Designed and Published by:

The International & Public Relations Office,

The University of Manchester

"Those who aim at the true end of education - the discipline of the mind and the strengthening of its faculties for after use in the noblest way - they, too, will gain their end, for the very effort, if honestly made, implies success."

So ended the first lecture given at Owens College by Professor Greenwood, on a rainy Thursday, 13 March, 1851. Principal Scott, who was due to give the opening address, was indisposed on the big day. At the close of the first academic session in the following June, twenty-five students had been enrolled.

The Quay Street premises of Owens College were originally the home of Richard Cobden. He was the MP for Stockport and a prominent figure in the repealing of the Corn Laws. The building was presented to the College in 1854, by the Chairman of the Owens Endowment Trustees, George Faulkner. Despite being the friend who reputedly persuaded John Owens to invest his wealth in education, Faulkner does not have so much as a present day refectory dining room named after him!

Conditions at Quay Street were less than ideal. At the time, the location was one of the most squalid and disreputable quarters of the city, and all approaches were via filthy alleys and poverty-stricken individuals. Classrooms were crowded, and the surroundings were cold and depressing; but this did not stop horse play in the students' room, who found entertainment by throwing chairs at one another. The cramped environment would have satisfied Owens's wish that his endowment should secure efficiency of teaching, rather than sufficiency of accommodation.

When the College moved to its present site in 1873, the building was subsequently used as a County Court, and is now being refurbished as office accommodation. A blue plaque records its famous past.

1908

The first building to grace what is now the Front Quad, was formally opened on 7 October, 1873 by the Duke of Devonshire. The construction work, executed by Messrs Clay and Son, began in 1870, on the four acre site bounded by Oxford Road, Burlington Street and Coupland Street, which had been purchased for £29,100. The architect was Alfred Waterhouse, who also designed Manchester Town Hall and The Royal Courts of Justice in London.

Waterhouse exhibited his design for the Owens College Quad at the Royal Academy in 1872. Although quite different from what emerged (a painting of the scheme hangs in the Owens Committee Room), the resultant buildings adhered to the Gothic Revivalist style which he planned.

Much debate was given to the design, not least to whether the first phase should front Oxford Road or be set back. In this context, the positioning of the clock seems unusual, as one would imagine that the tower beside the Whitworth Hall was a more appropriate location.

Like its neighbours, the John Owens Building is constructed of Darley Dale sandstone with terracotta roof tiling. It must have been quite a contrast for the students who moved there from the cramped accommodation on Quay Street. It is hard to dislike the style of the building, but one ex-student, commenting in 1901, considered the interior as being more like a public bathing establishment than a college, and opined that this was the reason for the lack of jollity in the new home.

1908

22 June, 1898, was a date of significance in the completion of the buildings around the front quadrangle. On this day, the Duke of Devonshire opened the Christie Library and laid the foundation stone for the Whitworth Hall.

The Hall was constructed, using funds of £50,000 from the bequest of Sir Joseph Whitworth, an engineer famed for his work on the standardisation of the screw thread. Following the scheme begun by Alfred Waterhouse, the Hall was completed under the direction of his son Paul, and provided a much needed venue for ceremonials and other large gatherings.

The opening ceremony was conducted on 12 March, 1901, fifty years to the day since the opening of Owens College. The damp and gloomy weather on the day was lightened by the high spirits of the undergraduates gathered in the Quad. A metaphorical sun must have shone when the Prince and Princess of Wales arrived to conduct the inauguration.

The appearance of the Hall today is a credit to those charged with its maintenance, as it appears virtually unchanged from this Edwardian view. However, in the intervening 80-odd years, several significant developments have taken place. For example, the mighty organ, which was a gift from Mrs Rylands, was largely rebuilt in 1962. The ornate chandeliers of today, virtually identical in appearance to the ones seen here, were actually rescued from the redundant Church of the Saviour in Bolton. They were fitted in the early 1970s to replace pendant floodlights fitted some 40 years previously.

1897

The University community is privileged to have the third-largest academic library in the UK at its disposal. However, as with many things, it is from little acorns that mighty oak trees grow.

This picture shows the cramped facilities available to the class of 1897. Conditions improved the following year when the Christie Library opened and facilities were further expanded in 1937, when the first phase of the present library site opened as the home of the Arts collection.

The original library was located on the top corridor of the main building. The foreground of this view is now the Student Records Office and the space visible in the background is divided into the Academic Secretary's Secretary's (sic) Office and a ladies toilet.

The keen eyed will note that the library divided the top corridor into two sections, hence the doors on the left and right of the picture. Evidence of the split still exists today in the swathe of grey lino, which interrupts the decorative floor tiles at this site.

FIRST FLOOR PLAN

GROUND FLOOR PLAN.

The stylishly redeveloped Christie Building has rightly been awarded a number of prestigious prizes for its adaptation into office space for the University's outreach activities. If the development depicted here had gone ahead, you could avoid getting wet on the journey from the John Owens Building.

The Christie Library was opened in 1898 by the Duchess of Devonshire and provided much needed space for the then huge collection of 70,000 books. Contemporary etchings and photographs show that the bridge was still being contemplated even then, as protruding masonry allowed for its addition. The original plans show the bridge, although it is marked "This portion is not included in the present contract".

If the plan had gone ahead, it would have necessitated the addition of a small extension to the John Owens Building, to provide stair access at two levels. Because of extensive internal modifications in the 1950s, it is now hard to visualise where this access would have been gained.

With hindsight it is a pity that the plan was shelved, as it would have neatly closed off the front quad, although modern lorries would no doubt have had difficulty entering. Evidence of the project remains on the staircase by the Christie Bistro, a stained glass window filling the space where the bridge would have been attached. Similarly buttresses still exist by the front entrance door, which were designed to support the arch.

At the turn of the century, the Senate Comittee room served as common room for women students. This atmospheric picture is redolent of a television costume drama; one can almost hear a clock ticking in the background.

It is hard nowadays to comprehend the segregation of the sexes that existed then, even in such a liberal educational environment.

John Owens founded the University with a bequest of £96,654. Despite being a Liberal and a Dissenter, he "was not fond of the society of ladies", and never married. When the College opened in 1851, despite being devoid of the religious hindrances imposed at the older Universities, it was a men-only establishment. It was not until 1883 that a Department for Women was formed, although unofficial lecture courses for women had been given before this date. The Court of Governors of the College resolved in 1877, that it was

"not prepared to sanction the principle of mixed education, believing that this would be at once opposed to the true educational interests of students of either sex, and out of harmony with the sentiments and usages of society."

The Court did, however, assist in the formation of a College for Women, housed at 225 Brunswick Street (nowadays the site of the Simon Building), whose courses were taught by Owens staff and, following amalgamation, formed the Department for Women. By the turn of the century most classes were mixed sex, and females were even allowed to study medicine from 1899. The first female graduate of the Medical School, Catherine Chisholm, was later to marry John Stopford, Vice-Chancellor from 1934 - 1956, after whom the Medical School is named.

1908

Medical training has a long and distinguished history in Manchester, beginning with the lectures in Anatomy and Physiology given by Charles White from 1783. Roget, who found fame with his thesaurus, taught Physiology in the city from 1806, and a School of Anatomy was founded by Joseph Jordan in 1814. The man who set in motion the amalgamation of the various teaching institutions in the city was Thomas Turner, FRCS, who founded the Manchester School of Medicine in 1824. His efforts culminated in the then Manchester Royal School of Medicine becoming a part of Owens College in 1873.

The timing coincided with the opening of the Oxford Road premises, and the building in the foreground was one of the original College group. This explains why reference is sometimes made to the "Old" rather than "Back" Quad, as it predates by thirty years the more familiar square beside the Whitworth Hall, which was only completed at the turn of the century.

Designed by Waterhouse, and costing £12,000 to build, the premises were opened by Thomas Huxley in 1874. The energetic men (are there any other kind?) who ran the School, were soon expanding their empire, and in 1894 the large extension visible in the background was opened. Professor John Morgan was largely responsible for ensuring the granting of the Medical Charter in 1883, which allowed the new Victoria University to award medical and surgical degrees.

Always at the forefront of the discipline, Manchester's many "firsts" include the opening in 1892, of the first Public Health Laboratory by Sheridan Delepine, and the appointment of Julius Dreschfeld as the first Professor of Pathology in Britain.

1908

Considering the significance of the work performed there, Coupland I and its memorial plaques could never be cautioned for undue trumpet blowing. Eminent scientists who worked there, included Geiger, Niels Bohr, Bragg, Chadwick, Rutherford - who, in 1919, split the atom on these premises - and Williams and Kilburn - who built the first stored program computer here in 1948. A list of such famous names makes it astonishing to think, that this sedate Victorian building has housed some of the greatest scientific minds of the 20th century.

Two anonymous gifts totalling £15,000 provided the means for the new laboratories to be built. The state-of-the-art facility that opened in 1901 owed a lot to the shrewdness of Arthur Schuster and the architect J.W. Beaumont, who had undertaken a European tour to see what their peers had at their disposal. The crowning glory of the new building was a domed observatory with 10 inch refracting telescope, which must have struggled with the murky atmosphere of the time. The octagonal base of this structure is now used to keep bees, the dome having long since been removed. When this photograph was taken the Museum extension and the end piece of the John Owens Building had yet to be built.

The bench on which Rutherford performed his famous experiment is still intact, as is the room that contained the enormous Manchester Mark 1 computer. Plans have yet to be devised for the Coupland I Science Theme Park

The 1970's decor of the Postgraduate Bar, with the passage of time, is now something of a historical item in itself, and would not look out of place in an episode of "The Likely Lads". Its present incarnation hides the fact that it was originally used for the more sober pursuit of chemical research, as depicted here.

The Schunk Building has a fascinating history in that it was originally sited in Kersal and was re-erected at its present site in 1904. To confuse matters further, it was re-erected as a mirror image of the original, so that its staircase met up with the adjacent buildings on Burlington Street.

Edward Schunk, FRS, had studied Chemistry in Germany and came to Manchester to work in the family calico printing works. He retired from the business at an early age so that he could pursue his scientific studies, which were principally concerned with the properties of colouring matters. In 1876 he discovered anthraflavic acid, and subsequently devised a method for preparing chlorophyll in the pure state. In 1899 he was awarded the Davy medal of the Royal Society and the DSc of this University.

The building was designed according to Schunk's own specification, and served as both a museum of specimens and a practical workplace. The former library on the first floor is still largely intact, and features light oak panelling and signs of the zodiac around the ceiling.

A very early aerial photograph of the University, looking north - east over what was then a predominantly residential area. The familiar structures visible, apart from the front quad complex, include the Arts building, the cluster of buildings around the back quad and the three Couplands, although the centre section of "II" is yet to be built. The absence of the final piece of the Museum extension implies that the picture was taken before 1926.

Other notable landmarks include the cluster of buildings that constituted the refectories and Students' Union (between Burlington Street and Lime Grove); Dover House (on the corner of Dover Street and Oxford Road); on the left side of the picture, beside the Schunk Building, can be seen what was a brewery; on the other side of Burlington Street, the flat, curved roof of the University Garage (prop. Miss Verity) is visible.

Following the demolition in the 1960s of the houses in this locality, the loss of community is regrettable. However, it is well documented that many of them were in a deplorable state. It is a shame that the radical ideas for new housing to replace them were not a success.

Looking most appropriate for the blackout conditions, the Whitworth Hall presents a dark and menacing outline in this November view down Oxford Road. A military flavour is provided by the tractor unit on the right of the picture and the uniformed man crossing Dover Street.

In terms of physical damage, the University escaped lightly from World War II. A stick of incendiaries fell on the old Medical School (Coupland III) and a land mine dropped into the McDougall Centre swimming pool, but failed to explode. Hostilities caused the introduction of a four term year, to speed up the training of scientists and technologists, and staff and students collaborated in blackout and fire watching exercises, as well as manning the University Fire Brigade.

There is a wealth of detail in this picture, but the overall blackness of the image makes some of it hard to decipher. Oxford Road is cobbled and tram-tracked (note the vehicle poking out from Burlington Street); the traffic refuge is graced with an art deco "Keep Left" sign and a brace of swan-necked gas lights. A pair of substantial-looking prams are being pushed towards the city-centre.

1944

"A well-equipped and comfortable library is a place where one adds to one's stock of knowledge by assimilating information through active and not passive reading, by reading not automatically, but critically. It is even a place in which one discovers the tonic refreshment of browsing."

The University Librarian, Moses Tyson, wrote these words in 1936, in a small descriptive work about his new baby. With an initial capacity for 300,000 volumes, the library was extended in a harmonious style in the 1950's to form a U-shaped complex. The polygonal Muriel Stott Conference Centre was added in the late 1970s, and immediately afterwards the massive new block and entrance hall was tacked on, cutting off Burlington Street in the process.

The interior of the original building is still intact and is a delight, featuring the clean lines so typical of the period when it was built. Note the Travertine facings covering the lower sections of the wall, which are both stylish and save on redecoration costs into the bargain.

Before the new entrance was built, the counter depicted here would have been a hive of activity, it being in close proximity to the main doorway. In those pre-electronic good-old days, measures to counteract book theft included a supervised wicket gate and the banning of bags and cases from being brought into the library. However, crime fears were not, it seems, of great magnitude then, as Dr Tyson felt "confident that the number of black sheep among our student readers is not unduly large."

The Students' Union Coffee Bar

It's ten to three in the afternoon, early November 1944, and a cheerful looking bunch of students take a break in the ecclesiastical splendour of the old Students' Union coffee bar.

The building stood on the Lime Grove side of what is now the refectory concourse. It started life as a Welsh Chapel, but with the expansion of the University was gradually encroached upon by the Students' Union and Refectory buildings. The inevitable take-over occurred in the 1930s, and for the last 20-odd years of its life 'Caf' provided that essential social service of any union coffee bar.

There was talk in 1925 of acquiring the chapel as a new Women's Union, so that the men could take over the existing female facilities on the Oxford Road frontage. This evoked a storm of outrage in Serpent (the Union newspaper), including a diatribe from a writer called 'Ajax', who dismissed the need for more space, and derided the women student activists as "Rawboned Amazonian giants with the stature of dragoons, the bull necks and brawny arms of the professional pugilist, and the language of the Billingsgate porter; crop-eared colossi, reeking with tobacco smoke and aggressively talking at the tops of their voices in a ringing baritone, they present an appearance in every way superlative; one hundred percent he-man."

This picture was taken six months before the end of the second world war, hence the majority of women.

Staff House - The Men's Room

An image for which the words "frightfully British" immediately spring to mind, this picture shows the minimalist splendour that was the men's room of Staff House.

Built in 1937 to a design by the architects Thomas Worthington & Sons, Staff House stood on the site of what is now the refectory concourse. As with the old Students' Union, men and women were allocated separate rooms in the building.

The photograph was taken professionally and, since this would involve some posing and placing of props, may explain the slightly self-conscious appearance of the chaps. It may also explain why Mr Kaye, the Bursar (semi-upright, bald head, right of picture), who was not known as a fashion guru, has a copy of "Vogue" on his lap; his attention is taken by the weighty tome held by his colleague, Mr Rainford. To the right of the fireplace H F Grundy (Pharmacy) is ignoring the copy of "Fortnightly Review" lying on the table. Beside him, J B M Herbert (Chemistry) is reading "Time & Tide", a long defunct weekly news journal.

With the second world war still raging, a military presence is provided by F/O E Howell of the Air Squadron, and A W G Ewing (Deaf Education, second left) appears to be using a tank trap as an occasional table.

1944

The stylish decor of the Women's Room echoes that of the men's, but there are some detail differences between the two. The fireplace on the right of the picture is less substantial than that provided for the chaps, and the club armchairs are upholstered in fabric rather than green leather. The round tables benefit from fresh flowers, which were absent from the square tables provided for the men.

The clock reads twenty five to eleven, and the room is graced with the presence of Miss Mainfroy (French), Miss Shaw (Museum) and Miss Edwards (Botany), the latter two enjoying a magazine article during their mid-morning break. Note again the copy of *Vogue* lying on the table. It is interesting to note the majority of smokers, probably taking heed of Celia Johnson's remark in Brief Encounter that "women smoking in public is ghastly."

Staff House met with the bulldozers in the mid 1960s, to make way for the refectory concourse development. However, the wood panelling was removed at the request of the then Bursar, Mr Rainford, and still graces the walls of the senior common room.

"Bells Peal, Crowds Cheer Queen: Police Swept Aside. Radiant in Powder Blue."

So ran the headline of the Manchester Evening News on 31 May, 1951, when Queen Elizabeth visited the University as part of the centenary celebrations of the founding of Owens College.

Arriving by train at Victoria, the Queen proceeded amidst "flags and fluttering bunting, pealing bells and all the flowers of spring (which) transformed the grey buildings of Manchester into a scene of colour and gaiety as she drove through packed streets to honour the city's University in its centenary week."

Wearing a loose coat over a blue crepe dress with tucked bodice, peep-toed platform shoes and a grey fox fur, the Queen arrived at a packed front quad to be greeted by the guard of honour depicted here, which consisted of members of the University's OTC, Air Squadron and Women's Royal Army Corps.

The Queen, who was escorted throughout by Chancellor Woolton and Vice-Chancellor Stopford, visited the department of Deaf Education and the Arts Library, received an honorary LLD and went on to plant a commemorative tree at Ashburne Hall, before rejoining the Royal Train and undertaking an engagement in Liverpool.

Other news in this week of 1951 included a mining disaster at Easington Colliery, Geoff Duke lapping the TT course at 93 mph on a Norton, and the minimum admission price to football league matches being raised to one and sixpence. For a few more bob you could buy a new-fangled TV set and watch "Made by Hand: Stained Glass" followed by "The Amazing Dr Clitterhouse" (repeat).

1951

Training in the art of dentistry has been given at a range of locations in Manchester over the last two centuries. The first homes for the Dental School were buildings in the All Saints area. In 1908 the School moved to its first purpose-built facility, the Queen Anne style building, that now serves as the Museum extension on Oxford Road. In the early 1970s this fine building nearly met with the bulldozers as it was initially thought that converting it for the purposes of the Museum would not be possible. A replacement along the lines of the C & A store in Chester was envisaged!

The Turner Dental School derives its name from its major benefactor, who was a partner in the Turner & Newall manufacturing combine. It dates originally from 1940 and is notable for its Odeon-esque architectural style, which is unique on the University campus. World War II prevented the completion of the square structure we know today. When it was completed, the missing link depicted here, was first used as the home of the School of Architecture. The quadrangle was originally used as a car park, but has now been developed into the "Cons Clinic".

Despite modernisation of some parts of the building, notably the patient reception areas, much of the original internal features of the building still survive. An excellent series of archive photographs of the site, including the pawnbrokers that used to stand at the top of Coupland Street, can be seen on the staircase leading from the staff entrance.

1951

This September view neatly sums up just how much the expansion of the University in the late fifties and early sixties totally transformed the local neighbourhoods of Greenheys and Chorlton-on-Medlock.

The photograph was taken from near the west wing of the Arts Building, looking south. The road in the foreground is Ducie Street (now reduced to the cul-de-sac beside the Ducie Arms), and these days the octagonal NEAB building sits on the site of the garage and the buildings behind it. Cecil Street is the road on the right; the white building (the Leicester Hotel) and its neighbours have made way for a car park. On the horizon can be seen the stands and floodlights of Maine Road and the two churches which still stand on Lloyd Street.

A compulsory purchase order in 1960 sealed the fate of these buildings. The owner of the garage (Central Autos) raised an objection to the order, alas to no avail. At the time this picture was taken he was looking after a trio of Bedford OB buses and selling Cleveland petrol.

Maine Road played host to United on the sixth of the month, City taking the points with goals from Don Revie and Johnny Hart.

The Back Quadrangle

Looking at the non-descript car park that is today's back quad it is hard to imagine that these two whoppers once graced the scene, albeit for only a short time.

The back quad was home (from 1886) to the Chemistry department's Levenstein Laboratory. This building was subsequently extended and served as the engineering laboratories until 1907, when the Whitworth Engineering Laboratories (now known as Coupland II) were opened. The addition (in 1911) of the final part of the main building, meant that the building had to be demolished. The only remnant to survive was the chimney and boiler house, seen on the right of this picture.

The boiler provided steam heating for the adjacent buildings. It must have been well built because it was not replaced until 1946, when four Daniel Adamson double pass economic boilers (with 80 tube Senior Economiser) were installed. In 1951, an extension including the new chimney on the left, was built. When it was topped out, some young blighter scaled the chimney and painted the legend "Frying Tonight" on the brickwork.

Up until 1962, the boiler was coal fired. The coming of the Clean Air Act resulted in conversion to oil firing which brought along improved efficiency. In 1973, the chimney and associated buildings were demolished and replaced by car parking, steam for heating being now provided by the Precinct Centre and Humanities boiler houses.

1950s

Looking south-east from the old Medical School (Coupland III), this mid-1950's view shows the University Library undergoing one of its earlier extensions, and what existed before the last phase of the building was constructed in the late 1970s.

The flat roofed buildings in the foreground are the Lapworth Laboratories. On the other side of Burlington Street (which was a through route in those days) are the similar Robert Robinson Laboratories. Constructed in 1950, both buildings used to belong to the Chemistry Department which, until it moved to its new home in Brunswick Street in the 1960s, occupied most of the buildings on the north side of Burlington Street.

The Schunk Laboratory (home of the Postgraduate Society) is on the left and provides a reference point. The Arts Building can be seen in the left background, with the old home of Deaf Education in front of it.

The library extension seen here deserves credit for the way that it harmonises with the 1936 building. When the original was planned (on the lines of the Radcliffe extension at Oxford), it made allowance for a three fold extension to eventually accommodate one million books. This was part of a grand plan in which the library "would form a corner stone of a range of buildings devoted to the prosecution of arts studies, which will group themselves round it in a way not unlike the layout of an Oxford or Cambridge quadrangle."

The Lapworth Labs were demolished in 1971 and the site is now covered by the library entrance area. The Dixon Laboratories on the left still survive, although they are not now used for the study of chemistry.

1958

Prior to its recent refurbishment, the last major upheaval on the refectory site came in 1958 when the old Students' Union building was demolished to make way for the well known concrete and glass edifice.

Opened in 1908, the old Union was divided for all its 50 year existence into male and female sections (with separate entrances on Lime Grove and Burlington Street). It was one of the venues for the "Owens-Tech battle" of 1928-9, in which "exuberant" students engaged in fighting and vandalism to such an extent that it was reported as a riot in the American press, and scandalised the whole of the north west.

The old Union fronted a motley collection of buildings, including refectories, staff house and the converted Welsh chapel, which served as a student coffee bar.

At the time this picture was taken, Burlington Street was still a through route. Particular points of note are the soot-covered stone, the Morris saloon car and the trolleybus wires.

"Did you spill my pint?" A casual glance at this photograph draws the viewer to the two men in the left foreground, who appear to be squaring up to one another. Closer inspection indicates, that they are more likely to be having a heated intellectual debate, although it should be noted that the stem of a pipe is being brandished by the man on the right.

This row of houses, known simply as 242-262 Oxford Road, was earmarked as the site for the new Union in the early 1950s. Although they were originally private dwellings, the houses did have University connections at various times: Number 248 served as the Women's Union until 1908, when new premises were built on what is now the site of the Refectory, and the building on the extreme right was the home of the School of Architecture from 1922. The Speeresque union building that now stands on the site opened in 1958.

The letters "EWS" painted on the wall in the foreground are a relic of the War, standing for "Emergency Water Supply." Note also the design of the lamp post, a style which has been copied on the new installations on Oxford Street.

As long ago as 1947 the University was talking in "super" superlatives about a new utopian student paradise to sweep away all memories of the gloomy Burlington Street home of the Students' Union.

This picture shows the naked skeleton of the new building on a glorious June day, in 1956. Note the long-gone Avondale Hotel and secretarial college to the left of the Holy Name church, and the three-wheeler car in the foreground.

The general layout of the new building was for separate men's and women's sections but with more extensive joint facilities than before; allowance was made for the possibility of a fully mixed union, although at the early stages of planning there was no such demand for this.

Perhaps because of the inevitable compromise in the design, a group of architecture students produced, in 1954, a critical report which summarised that "the basic fault (of the building) seems to be in the circulation, or arrangement of rooms to each other, and service corridors and halls... there appears little logic in the arrangement of the structure either. We seriously consider the design lacking in any feeling towards a conception of the importance or use of the University Union and the faults in planning seem so basic that nothing but a complete re-appraisal of the requirements and a new design could satisfy the alterations and adjustments envisaged. It is symbolic that in the entire scheme, nothing seems worthy of retention as a positive good arrangement or idea."

After careful consideration of the points raised by the architecture students, work on the building proceeded unchanged and the new premises opened in the 1957-58 academic session.

"Few members of staff venture into the Students' Union without a specific invitation... casual and uninitiated contact is much less likely to occur there than in either the refectory or department."

The above comment, as valid today as when it first appeared in March 1962, featured in a survey of Staff-Student relations at the University which is full of similarly timeless comments. In an age of 'quality' and 'customer service' it is heartening to know that the University was encouraging student feedback more than 30 years ago.

The staff of that era would consequently have missed out on the delights of the glittering new Union building, which was opened by Harold Macmillan in 1958. The picture shows the pristine entrance foyer, complete with the flying saucer lamp shades, "Christine Keeler" armchairs and angled door pushes so redolent of the era.

Much effort was made to retain the "club" atmosphere of the old union in the new place, even to the extent of the Union Steward (Arthur Nichol) wearing morning dress whilst on duty. However, the expansion of higher education and consequent increase in student numbers brought this way of life to an end.

The foyer, though still recognisable today, has been much modified since the picture was taken - an enquiry desk and travel agents fill the background area, and the linoleum floor has been succeeded by carpet.

The casual observer would be forgiven for thinking that the 'back entrance' to the Christie Building was anything other than part of the original development of buildings around the front quad. However, this view shows the newly emergent extension to the then Science Library rising beside the evidently long-established and soot-blackened Whitworth Hall.

It is pleasing to note the harmony of the extension's architecture with its distinguished neighbours. Note also the still extant Edwardian lamp bracket on the right of the picture, in front of what is now the fire escape exit door to the Christie Building.

Now that all the orginal main buildings are recognisable as being built of sandstone (cleaning took place in the early 1970's), the only points that distinguish the extension as being 'different' are the less weathered masonry details and the slightly lighter shade of stone in its walls.

1957

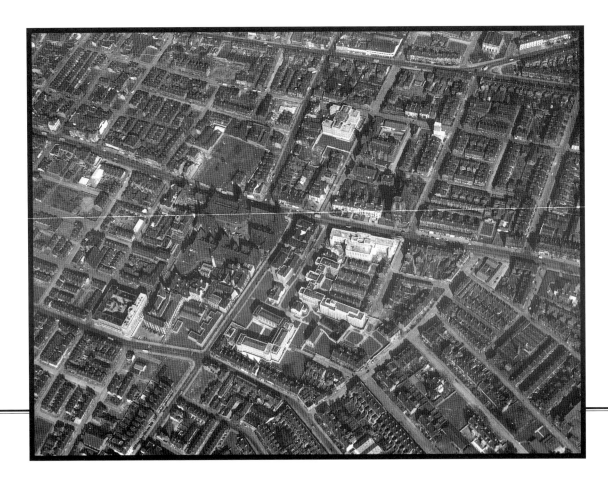

Athough, compared to the photograph of the campus in the 1920s, a number of additions have been made to the University's building stock in the intervening 30 years, this picture shows how relatively compact the site was, even at the end of the 1950s. The Robbins Report, which precipitated a major expansion of the University sector, began the change in appearance of the campus, to that which we know today.

Notable new buildings visible in this view, include: the Electrical Engineering building on Dover Street; the Students' Union building, nearing completion on Oxford Road; the then recently enlarged Arts Library, and the West Wing of the Arts building. Beside the latter is the "T" shaped building that served as an extension to the Arts building from 1948.

Although the first appearance of open spaces surrounding University buildings is evident, there are still huge numbers of terraced houses encroaching the campus. Note Leamington and Blossom Streets tightly hemmed in between Arts and the Students' Union. Other pleasantly named roads which are visible but now obliterated include Enfranchise Place, Mahogany Street and Honduras Street.

1960

The recognition of the University campus as the stamping ground of Frederick Engels, is rightly commemorated with a blue plaque at the Whitworth Park residences. However, his residence and the visits of his collaborator Karl Marx, extended far beyond 6 Thorncliffe Road.

Engels was wealthy enough to have a great deal of rented accommodation at his disposal, for the use of both himself and his friends. Marx is recorded as having visited on 20 occasions and stayed at many addresses in this area including 17 Burlington Street, 58 Dover Street and 27 Cecil Street.

Dover House stood on the corner of Oxford Road and Dover Street and served as the headquarters of the Albert Club, of which Engels was an active committee member in the 1850s. It was one of many social clubs, catering for the then large expatriate German population.

From 1893 to 1908 the building served as the men's Student Union, (the original Union stood on the site of the Christie Building). Women students had the use of 248 Oxford Road, which stood on the site of the present Union.

In its final incarnation, for the 40 years up to 1962, Dover House served as the headquarters of the JMB. When they moved out, the building was demolished.

Of particular note in this 1960 view are the cranes, busy constructing the Simon Building, and the assortment of vehicles, including a BSA pre-unit twin motorcycle and Nash Metropolitan car, parked beside what is now the Nat West Bank.

1960

Photographed from the Coupland Street archway, this view shows the commercial properties, which included a Post Office and Fieldens the Stationers, that were swept aside by the construction of the Maths tower and, latterly, the Computer building. The flat-roofed building on the right of the picture still exists, and provides a reference point. Originally the home of Brookes' Wireworks, it was taken over by the University, and following extension work, was used as the linear accelerator laboratory until relatively recently.

The Maths tower of today represents the visible starting point of the grandiose plans for the Manchester Education Precinct which never saw completion. In essence this sought to link the educational institutions stretching from UMIST in the north, to the teaching hospitals on Oxford Road. The precinct would ultimately achieve " a comprehensive approach to Higher Education to meet the needs of a wide range of students....and a site so close to the city centre lends itself to the possibility of a significant fusion of town and gown."

Although the precinct theme has recently been revived, it does not bear comparison with the brutalist scheme envisaged thirty years ago. An essential part of this scheme, that of elevated walkways to separate humans from traffic, still exists around the fulcrum of the project, the Precinct Centre, with its inconveniently located first floor shopping centre. That other familiar example of deck access building, the Hulme flats, used the same group of planning consultants.

The Williamson Building is named after Mr WC Williamson, Professor of Natural History, Botany and Geology. He was one of the original group of five professors who commenced teaching duties at the Quay Street home of Owens College in 1851.

The building that bears his name was the first of the new group of science buildings to be erected along Brunswick Street. The first phase of the Williamson, the Oxford Road frontage, opened in the late 1950's, subsequent wings being added during the following decade. When it opened, the mathematics department was the first tenant, although their stay was to last less than ten years with their departure to the newly completed tower block next door.

This 1959 view shows the departmental library on the third floor, still displaying that "just opened" look. The four men in the picture are all exponents of the tweed jacket and flannels look and seem to be working jolly hard, as do the two women in the background. The room fittings are typically 1950s in style, and somebody appears to have gone mad with a spirograph in designing the patterns on the glass panels.

1960

If you fancied shaking a leg of a Friday evening, there was a time when these desires could be fulfilled by a short stroll up Brunswick Street, to the bright yellow stuccoed palace that was Shorrocks Dance Hall.

Shorrocks, which stood in front of the Electrical Engineering building (visible in the background), featured a grandiose neo-classical entrance porch reminiscent of that on the Arts building. However, in comparison to that sober centre of learning, this entertainment Mecca (perhaps appropriately) always looked as though it had overdone it on the make-up.

As with many of the local centres of entertainment, Shorrocks was popular with the Irish community, who used to live in the neighbourhood. Long-serving members of the current University staff can still recall tales about the place, and it seems that then, as now, the cocktail of lads, drink and music was a sure-fire recipe for a punch-up.

This June view is looking south from what today is the lawn beside the Williamson Building . The road in the foreground, New York Street, used to run parallel to Oxford Road and was obliterated by the development of the University. The parked vans show what the Ford Transit has deprived us of over the last thirty years.

When the building was being demolished to make way for the grassland of today, there was a mass exodus of rats, from nests which they had built in the benches inside the hall. How long they had been there is anybody's guess, but you can still see their relatives in the shrubs on the East side of Oxford Road.

The Academy, which opened in 1990, is one of Manchester's leading concert venues and provides the Students' Union with much needed extra accommodation. However, as this 1960 view shows, the students of today are not the first to pursue pleasure on this site.

The term "Gin Palace" is most appropriate for the Kings Hotel, seen on the left of the picture. Elaborate public houses seem more prevalent in Liverpool than Manchester, so it is fitting that the Kings Hotel served Higsons Ales, which used to be brewed in Toxteth. Despite the grandiose exterior, the inside of the hostelry was plain, but it did boast a stage and, and in combination with the largely Irish clientele, was good for a sing-song of an evening.

The whole of this site had been earmarked as the home of an extension to the Students' Union building for many years - the plans for the Stopford Building included provision of an overhead walkway to access the new wing. Numerous proposals came and went as finance for the new construction was not made available. Although, undoubtedly, a useful building, the lego-land Academy of today is a poor architectural successor to what used to prevail.

1960

This view is taken from what today is the exit of the Dover Street car park. Whereas today you can only turn right or left, in pre-Beatle days you could carry straight on to Booth Street and beyond along the now defunct Rumford Street.

The building depicted here, which is now the site of the Chemistry Building, was occupied by the Sisters of Charity of Saint Vincent de Paul, who in the 1920s, set up two hostels in association with the Holy Name Church. They also had the use of one of the large houses that used to stand on Upper Brook Street.

At the time the picture was taken there was an almost unbroken line of buildings up to Brunswick Street. As well as domestic dwellings, there also stood the workshop of S. Roland, furrier, whose premises, for the benefit of passers-by, bore the legend "MADAME! YOUR FUR NEEDS ATTENTION". In the very dark and distant past, Rumford Street was also home to both University staff and students, as well as the writer Elizabeth Gaskell, before she moved to what is now the International Society HQ on Plymouth Grove.

As seems to have been the way in the 1960s, the objections of the Trustees of the Sisterhood to the compulsory purchase of their premises, were not allowed to get in the way of University expansion. Progress also erased the through route, although the line it once took either side of Brunswick Street can still be seen

1960

Once upon a time, before the advent of supermarkets and motoring for the masses, this country was a "Nation of Shopkeepers". Our densely populated inner cities depended on them for everything from a tin of beans to a quarter of humbugs.

This particular example stood on the site of what are now the entrance gates to the Chemistry Building. The road on the right nowadays serves as a parking area. Brunswick Street in the foreground is still a through route, although its closure and pedestrianisation has been on the agenda for a very long time.

The picture is an interesting sociological snapshot of how we used to live. The shop window display is promoting three brands of fizzy pop, four brands of filterless cigarette, and two brands of tea. Advertising agencies were obviously fond of alliteration at the time ("Players Please" , "Senior Service Satisfy"), but it is unlikely that they would get away with calling bread "Mothers Pride" in this day and age.

1960

Along with the Chemistry Building, the Schuster Laboratory forms the eastern limit of the copper roofed "science precinct" based along Brunswick Street. It was the last of these Fairhurst-designed buildings to be commissioned and provided much needed extra space for this large department.

This June view is looking down Upper Brook Street. The Morris van and Rover P4 are waiting for the traffic lights from Brunswick Street to change. Appropriately enough, "Fashion Corner" dominates the apex of the junction; next door is a newsagents/ tobacconists and beside that an electrical shop. Further down the street stood the Kashmir Indian restaurant. If you didn't fancy "that funny foreign food", the UCP restaurant was the place for you, just around the corner,.

Upper Brook Street resembled its parallel neighbour Oxford Road in being dominated by small shops, now largely erased by the redevelopment and road widening schemes of the sixties and seventies.

The Arthur Worthington Hall

The Dover Street home of the Economics Faculty has a very interesting history. This listed building designed by Mills & Murgatroyd and completed in 1886 originally housed the Manchester High School for Girls. The building was used by the Armed Forces in the Second World War as a recruitment centre and when in 1947 the High School moved to their new home in the leafy South Manchester suburbs, the recently founded School of Education moved in. The completion of the Humanities Building in the early 1960s meant another move for Education, and the Economics Faculty took over, remaining there to the present day.

The Arthur Worthington Hall shown here used to stand along what is now the entrance to the Dover Street car park. It was demolished to make way for the unharmonious extension to the Economics building, which was completed in 1967.

1960

The present home of the Royal Northern College of Music, on the corner of Booth Street West and Oxford Road, does not score highly in the beauty stakes, but has a pleasantly airy interior. Before its completion in the early 1970s, the then Manchester College of Music occupied these premises on Devas Street.

Handily situated for the nearby Kings Hotel, this large red brick pile included the attractive Lees Hall for in-house concerts and the like. The single storey building in the foreground, now the home of the Brickhouse Theatre Company, was custom built for the College in 1948, and incorporated practice rooms and small halls.

After the main building was vacated, it was occupied by a group of some 50 students and other young people. Re-christened "The Squat" it was used as a venue for various events and was eventually purchased from the College by the University, with a view to providing extra accommodation for student activities. This situation did not last for very long as the building was demolished and the site is now a car park.

The Centre for Deaf Education

Photographed from beside the old wing of the Library, the Moberly Tower provides easy reference for this site, which nowadays forms the goods entrance to the Refectory.

Educational work for the deaf began at the University in 1919, with the establishment of the Ellis Llywd Jones lectureship in education of the deaf. The first appointee, Irene Goldsack, was something of a radical who practised novel techniques which certainly caused controversy amongst the establishment. In 1922 she married Alexander Ewing, and the couple became one of the most famous teams in the sphere of Deaf Education.

Initially, Goldsack was allocated a "dark and gloomy" room in the top of the John Owens Building to train students in the discipline. Perhaps in part due to its prolific research output, the newly titled Department of Education of the Deaf moved into the premises depicted here in 1934. Previously used by the Fielden School, the new home featured both a sound proof room and a clinic, and served the department for over thirty years, before further University expansion allowed the next move to more spacious surroundings in the 1960's.

The Whitworth Hall and Holy Name Church provide easy reference points for this 29 year old view, which is both familiar, and yet shows how much things have changed in the intervening period.

It is August 1966, the sun is shining and England have just won the World Cup. Despite this the woman in the right foreground is looking a tad miserable - a West German fan perhaps?

The traffic on Oxford Road shows that congestion is nothing new. No less than three Mark 1 Ford Cortinas are visible, as well as a Vauxhall estate and an Austin taxi. On the left side of Oxford Road the long-gone row of shops can be seen. The grandiose building on the corner of Brunswick Street is Williams and Deacons Bank; facing it is the College Hotel, beside which is the building that used to serve as the Accommodation Office.

The signs in front of the Museum proudly proclaim that the new aquarium is now open, the blackened sandstone providing an effective backdrop - it would be a further six years before the buildings were blast cleaned to their original state.

The Holy Name Church

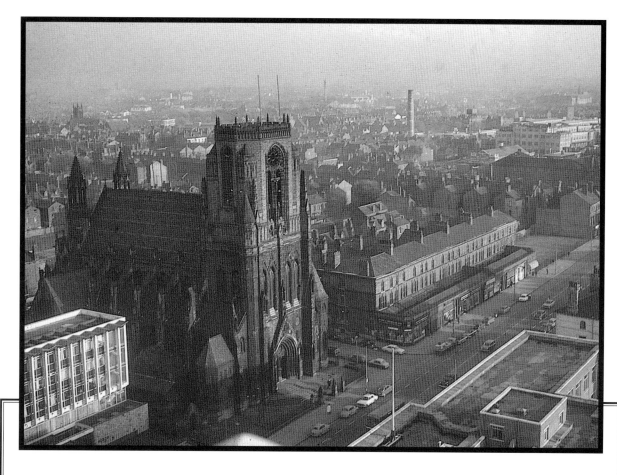

It is not easy to be enthusiastic about the Moberly Tower, whose dimensions overwhelm the original buildings grouped around the front quad. One of its saving graces, aside from providing student accommodation, is that it provides some excellent views across the city. This November view shows one of the most well-known landmarks in the area, the Holy Name Church, and some of its former neighbours, which have given way to the Medical School and the Academy.

The Holy Name is considered the finest church to have been designed by Joseph Hansom (of Hansom Cab fame). It was completed in 1871, and was originally to feature a steeple 240 feet high, which was never built. The familiar octagonal tower was actually added in 1928, as a memorial to Father Bernard Vaughan, an indomitable character who, amongst other things, raised the funds for the construction in 1890 of the adjacent church hall (now the Jabez Clegg pub). The tower was designed by Adrian Gilbert Scott, a member of that great architectural dynasty, which may explain its similarity with the structure on the Anglican Cathedral at Liverpool.

The then new chaplaincy building on Oxford Road, visible on the left of the picture, though not as decorative as its neighbour, also has connections with popular culture, since its architects, Mather & Nutter, were responsible for the cantilevered stands at Old Trafford football stadium.

The College Hotel

1973

The scaffolding poles are an ominous sign of things to come, as the demolition men prepare to reduce a much loved local landmark to rubble.

The College Hotel stood on the corner of Oxford Road and Brunswick Street, in front of the Williamson Building. As its name implies, the hostelry was open for business in the days when the University traded under another name, and early illustrations of the incomplete complex of buildings around the front quad bear witness to this.

In its original form, the College Hotel followed the architectural style of its neighbours. In the 1930s, the building was extensively altered and gained the sandstone facings seen here, thus complementing the grandiose buildings over the road. However, the adjacent buildings on Oxford Road, which ultimately included the Accommodation Office, retained their plain brickwork right up to the end.

Inevitably, given its location, the College was a popular haunt for both staff and students and provided an informal venue, apparently, for interaction between the two groups. It was also the Saturday lunchtime haunt of the 1950s City stars Roy Paul and Bobby Johnson, prior to their fortnightly performances at Maine Road.

As well as the memories of longer serving members of staff, there are also two physical reminders of the College still visible: In the shrubbery that now covers the site, is a piece of pub masonry carved with an eagle device, and incorporated in one of the internal walls of the computer building is a stone proclaiming "College Hotel," which was rescued from the site by some enterprising students, in collaboration with Estates and Services.